Books in First Steps Series

First Steps

The Bible Tells Me So

God Takes Care of Me

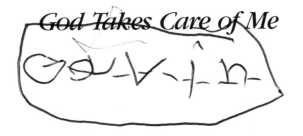

GOD TAKES CARE OF ME

75 Devotions for Families with Young Children

Paul J. Loth

Illustrated by
Daniel J. Hochstatter

THOMAS NELSON PUBLISHERS
Nashville • Atlanta • London • Vancouver

Published in Nashville, Tennessee, by Thomas Nelson, Inc., Publishers, and distributed in Canada by Word Communications, Ltd., Richmond, British Columbia.

The devotions in this publication are based on the Contemporary English Version. Copyright © 1991, 1992, 1995, American Bible Society.

ISBN 0-7852-7988-1

Printed in the United States of America.

1 2 3 4 5 6 — 00 99 98 97 96 95

Contents

An Open Letter to Parents

It is no secret that the lessons learned in the first five years of life are among the most significant lessons your children will ever learn.

As a parent, I have thought about that often. I want my children to love God, to understand His Word, and to follow Him. I think every Christian parent feels the same way. That is why Christian parents want to encourage their children to begin private devotions at a young age.

God Takes Care of Me helps your children understand God's love. God took care of many people throughout the pages of Scripture. As these individual stories are told, children are encouraged to think about how God takes care of them, too. Each devotional time is divided into four sections:

The Thinking Step Discussion questions help your children relate to the experiences of biblical characters. By thinking about related experiences in their own lives, your children will have a good opportunity to understand how they felt.

The Listening Step God's Word is truth. As children hear God's Word, they are led into the truth and can grow in the knowledge of God. During this second step in their devotions, children hear how God took care of His people in the Bible.

The Talking Step Learning takes place when there is interaction. After hearing God's Word, your children will have the opportunity to talk about ways in which they can apply God's truth to their lives.

The Praying Step Children can be guided in the development of their relationship with the heavenly Father. Your children will learn to talk with God as they would talk to a friend.

Encourage your children to memorize the short Bible verse that ends each devotion. Each verse relates directly to the theme of the devotional, and memorizing it helps keep the lesson with your children.

May your children's devotional time be a time in which they act on God's truth and grow in understanding of how God cares for them.

Paul J. Loth, Ed. D.

God Gave Adam a Beautiful Home

Genesis 2:8–17

❓ The Thinking Step

Do you like your home? Why?
    What is your favorite room? What do you like to do there?

👂 The Listening Step

Adam was the first person God made. God made a beautiful place for Adam to live. He gave Adam a nice home.

The Garden of Eden was Adam's home. It had many trees. It even had a big river. When Adam got hungry, all he had to do was eat something from one of the trees!

God thought of everything. Every beautiful tree was in the garden. Every tree with tasty fruit was there, too. And the river gave the trees plenty of water.

God let Adam take care of everything. God took good care of Adam.

🗣 The Talking Step

Name all the things God has given you.
    Why did He give them to you?

✋ The Praying Step

Thank You, God, for all You have given me. Thank You for taking such good care of me.

> The earth and everything on it belong to the LORD. The world and its people belong to him.
>
> —*Psalm 24:1*

God Gave Adam a Wife

Genesis 2:8–25

 ## The Thinking Step

Do you ever get lonely? Why?
    What do you do when you are lonely?
    Do you ask God to help you not be so lonely?

The Listening Step

God made Adam. He was the first man. God gave Adam a beautiful garden. The prettiest and the best trees were there.

God filled the garden with birds and animals. God brought all the animals to Adam. He let Adam name each one.

But Adam was lonely. God knew Adam needed someone who was like him.

So God gave Adam a wife. Adam named her Eve. Adam was not lonely anymore. God took care of him. Adam and Eve were very happy together.

The Talking Step

Name a time you were lonely and God helped you. What did God do?
    Thank God for giving you a family and friends to help you not be lonely.

✋ The Praying Step

Dear God, thank You for giving me a family and friends to help me not be so lonely. Help me remember that You are always with me.

> A friend is always a friend, and relatives are born to share our troubles.
>
> *—Proverbs 17:17*

God Protected Cain Even Though He Disobeyed

Genesis 4:1–15

The Thinking Step

When was the last time you disobeyed your parents?
Did they still love you? Did they take care of you? Why?

The Listening Step

Cain was not happy. Cain and his brother, Abel, brought offerings to God. God did not like what Cain brought. God liked what Abel brought better. That made Cain angry. Cain became so angry he killed Abel.

"Where is Abel?" God asked Cain one day. "How should I know?" Cain said. "Am I supposed to look after my brother?"

God knew what had happened to Abel. He knew Cain had killed him. So God punished Cain. "This punishment is too hard!" Cain pleaded with God. "Anyone could kill me." So God protected Cain. He put a special mark on Cain so anyone who saw him would not kill him.

Cain disobeyed God. He did a very bad thing. Even though God punished Cain, He still protected him. God kept Cain safe.

The Talking Step

Name a time you disobeyed God. Did He punish you? How?
Did God still take care of you? Why?

The Praying Step

Dear God, thank You for taking care of me. Thank You for always watching over me no matter how I might disobey You.

> The LORD protects his people, and they can come to him in times of trouble.
>
> –Psalm 37:39

God Kept Noah Safe

Genesis 6:1–8:1

 The Thinking Step

When was the last time you heard about something really bad happening to someone? What happened?

The Listening Step

God was not happy. Many people did not obey God. They did not love God. They made God very sad. "I'm sorry I ever made them," God said. "I'll destroy every living creature on earth!"

But Noah loved God. He tried to please God. God wanted Noah to be safe. He told Noah to build an ark, a big boat.

Noah and his family would live in the ark. The ark would keep them safe.

Soon it started to rain. Water fell from the sky all day and all night. Water was everywhere. But God kept Noah safe. Noah loved God. God watched over Noah and his family.

The Talking Step

Name a time God kept you safe.
Did you thank Him?

🖐 The Praying Step

Dear God, I know You keep me safe many times, and I do not even know it. Thank You for watching over me. Remind me that You watch over me.

> You were in serious trouble, but you prayed to the LORD, and he rescued you.
>
> —*Psalm 107:28*

God Saved Lot from His Enemies

Genesis 14:1–17

❓ The Thinking Step

Do you know people who are mean to you?
    What do they do that is mean?
    What can you do about it?

👂 The Listening Step

Do you have an uncle? Abram was Lot's uncle. Lot and his family lived in Sodom. Abram was nice to Lot. He tried to help him.

One day some men attacked Sodom. Many people who lived in Sodom ran for their lives. Others were taken prisoner. The men made Lot and his family prisoners. They even took everything away from Lot.

One of the people who escaped came to find Abram, Lot's uncle. He told Abram what had happened. Abram got all his men together. Then he went to rescue his nephew, Lot.

God saved Lot. He sent Abram to rescue Lot. Sometimes God sends people to save us, too.

The Talking Step

Name a time God saved you from people who acted mean.
    Did God use other people to help you?
    Did you thank them? Did you thank God?

🤲 The Praying Step

Dear God, thank You for protecting me. Thank You for letting other people help me. Help me always to remember to thank You.

> You are my mighty rock, my fortress, my protector, the rock where I am safe, my shield, my powerful weapon, and my place of shelter.
>
> —Psalm 18:2

God Gave Abram a Large Family

Genesis 15:1–16

The Thinking Step

Does your family get together at holidays?
Do some relatives live somewhere else?

The Listening Step

Abram loved God. He tried to obey God. God loved Abram, too. One night God spoke to Abram. He told him to go outside.

"Look at the sky and see if you can count the stars," God said. Abram looked up. There were so many stars he could not count them all.

"That's how many descendants you will have," God said.

Abram did not understand. God had not yet given him any children. But he believed God. Soon Abram and his wife had a son. His name was Isaac. Many more children and grandchildren were born, too. God changed Abram's name to Abraham, which means "father of many." God keeps His promises. We can always trust God.

The Talking Step

What did Abram do when God promised him a large family?
What should we do when God gives us a promise?
Name another promise God has given in the Bible. Has He kept it?

🖐 The Praying Step

Dear God, thank You for Your promises. Thank You for always keeping Your promises. Help me to trust You more.

Always let [God] lead you, and he will clear the road for you to follow.

—Proverbs 3:6

God Gave Isaac a Wife

Genesis 24:1–67

The Thinking Step

Who are your best friends? What do you like to do most with them?
Do you think God wants you to have nice friends?

The Listening Step

It was time for Isaac, Abraham's son, to get married. Abraham wanted Isaac to marry someone from Abraham's homeland. Abraham sent his servant back to the homeland.

As he stood by a well, Abraham's servant prayed to God, "Please let me find a wife for Isaac today." He knew that the young woman who gave him and his camels a drink would be the one God had chosen for Isaac.

Soon a beautiful young woman came to the well. The servant said to her, "Please let me have a drink of water."

The young woman gave him a drink. Then she said, "Now I'll give your camels all the water they want." The servant knew God had given Isaac a wife. The young woman's name was Rebekah. She and Isaac would be very happy together.

The Talking Step

Ask your mom and dad how they knew who God wanted them to marry.
What kind of person would God want you to marry?

The Praying Step

Dear God, thank You for giving me friends and a family. Thank You for giving me people to love.

May the LORD bless his people with peace and happiness and let them celebrate.

—*Psalm 64:10*

God Blessed Jacob

Genesis 32:22–32

📋 The Thinking Step

What does it mean that "God blesses people"?

👂 The Listening Step

One night Jacob was alone. A man wrestled with him. They kept wrestling and wrestling. They wrestled all night long.

The man said to Jacob, "Let go of me! It's almost daylight." But Jacob would not let him go. "You can't go until you bless me," Jacob told him. "Your name will no longer be Jacob. Your name will be Israel," the man said. Then the man blessed Jacob.

Jacob had twelve sons. Jacob's grandchildren became the nation of Israel. They were special to God. God did many wonderful things for them.

🔊 The Talking Step

How has God blessed people you know?
    Have you asked God to bless you?
    Have you thanked God for blessing you?

24

🖐 The Praying Step

Dear God, thank You for blessing us. Please bless me in my life. Help me to do the things that will please You.

> Pray that our LORD will make us strong and give us peace.
>
> —*Psalm 29:11*

25

God Kept Jacob Safe from His Brother

Genesis 33:1–17

The Thinking Step

When was the last time you did something mean to someone?
Did it make that person mad? Did he or she do something mean to you?
What was it? Did you deserve it?

The Listening Step

Jacob and Esau were twins. Esau was born first, so he was to get the family's special blessing. But Jacob cheated Esau out of the blessing. Esau was mad. Jacob ran away because he was scared of Esau.

Many years passed. Jacob and Esau were both adults. They had children of their own. One day Jacob saw Esau coming toward him. He had 400 men with him! Jacob was scared.

As soon as Esau saw Jacob, he opened his arms and hugged Jacob. The two brothers, Jacob and Esau, cried in each other's arms!

God protected Jacob. And He brought the two brothers back together.

The Talking Step

How did God keep Jacob safe?
Name a time God straightened out a problem between you and a family member or a friend.

![hand icon] The Praying Step

Dear God, help me to get along with my family and my friends. Help me to be kind to everyone. Thank You for helping me in my friendships.

Some friends don't help, but a true friend is closer than your own family.

—Proverbs 18:24

God Saved Joseph from His Brothers

Genesis 37:12–36

The Thinking Step

Has something ever happened to you that you thought was bad, but it turned out to be good?

What happened? How did it turn out good?

The Listening Step

Jacob had 12 sons. But Joseph was his favorite. That made Joseph's brothers very mad. They did not like Joseph. They wanted to teach him a lesson.

One day Joseph's brothers saw him coming. "Let's kill him and throw him into a pit," they said. But Reuben, the oldest brother, had a better idea. "Let's not kill him," Reuben said. "Just throw him into a dry well." So that is what Joseph's brothers did.

Soon the brothers saw a group of men traveling on camels. They sold Joseph to the men. They took Joseph with them to Egypt, a land far away.

God kept Joseph safe. His brothers wanted to kill him. But God had a better plan.

The Talking Step

Describe a time in your life when God turned something bad into something good.

Thank God for working His plan in your life.

28

🖐 The Praying Step

Dear God, thank You for always taking care of me. Sometimes I think things are bad, but in Your plan they are really good. Help me to trust You more.

> We know that God is always at work for the good of everyone who loves him.
>
> —*Romans 8:28*

God Took Care of Joseph in Egypt

Genesis 39:1–40:23

❓ The Thinking Step

Have you ever been punished for something you did not do? What happened? How did you feel?

👂 The Listening Step

Joseph was in Egypt, and God watched over him. He became a slave for Potiphar, a very important man.

One day Potiphar's wife became angry with Joseph. She made up a story about Joseph to get him in trouble. Joseph ended up in prison.

In prison Joseph made two new friends. One friend had been the king's chief cook. The other friend had been the king's personal servant. One night both men had dreams. They did not know what the dreams meant.

"Tell me what you dreamed," Joseph said to them. So they told Joseph their dreams. Then God gave Joseph the knowledge to tell the men what their dreams meant.

Joseph was in prison for something he did not do. While in prison, he was able to help the chief cook and the king's servant with their problems. Joseph loved God. And God let him help others.

🔊 The Talking Step

Can you think of a time something happened to you that seemed bad but turned into something good? What happened? Were you able to help someone else? Why?

The Praying Step

Dear God, thank You for taking such good care of me. Help me to always trust You, even when things look bad. I know You are still watching over me.

> You tried to harm me, but God made it turn out for the best, so that he could save all these people, as he is now doing.
>
> —*Genesis 50:20*

God Made Joseph the Leader in Egypt

Genesis 41:1–45

The Thinking Step

What do you do when you are having a bad day?

What is the best way to turn a bad day into a good day?

The Listening Step

Joseph was in prison in Egypt. There Joseph was able to help the king's servant and the king's chief cook. Later Pharaoh, the king of Egypt, had a dream he did not understand.

The servant remembered Joseph. "When we told him our dreams," he said to Pharaoh, "he explained what each of them meant."

So Pharaoh took Joseph out of prison.

Joseph explained Pharaoh's dream. He also told Pharaoh what to do about it.

"No one could possibly handle this better than Joseph," Pharaoh declared. Then he turned to Joseph. "You are now governor of all Egypt!" Pharaoh said.

God took Joseph from being a slave to governing the entire country. God took good care of him!

The Talking Step

Have you ever had a bad day turn into a good day? What happened?

How did God make the day become a good day?

32

👋 The Praying Step

Dear God, sometimes I have a bad day. Help me to trust You during those days and not become discouraged.

> Our LORD and our God, you are like the sun and also like a shield. You treat us with kindness and with honor, never denying any good thing to those who live right.
>
> *–Psalm 84:11*

God Watched Over Moses as a Baby

Exodus 2:1–4

The Thinking Step

When was the last time you were alone?
Could you have taken care of yourself if something had happened?
Were you scared? Why? Why not?

The Listening Step

The Egyptians were worried. The Israelites were having lots of children. Soon there would be more Israelites than Egyptians. The Egyptians were afraid the Israelites would take control of the land.

So the Egyptians made a rule. No more Israelite baby boys could be born. But one day an Israelite baby boy was born. His mother loved him very much. She did not tell the Egyptians about her baby. She hid him in her house.

When the mother could not hide her baby any longer, she had an idea. She placed him in a basket.

The baby's mother took him down to the river. She trusted in God. She knew God would take care of him.

God kept watch over her baby. Her baby would be named Moses. He would lead the Israelites out of Egypt.

The Talking Step

Name a time you were scared and alone. What did you do?
Did you know God was watching over you? How did you know?

✋ The Praying Step

Dear God, thank You for always watching over me. Thank You for watching over everyone. Help me not to be scared. Help me to know that You are watching over me.

> Don't be afraid. I am with you.
>
> *—Isaiah 41:10*

God Gave Moses a Nice Home

Exodus 2:1–10

The Thinking Step

What do you like most about your family?
  What do you like most about your home?

The Listening Step

Miriam watched the basket as it floated on the river. Her baby brother was in that basket. Her mother had put him in the basket to hide him from the Egyptians. Soon the daughter of Pharaoh, king of Egypt, came to the river. She saw the baby floating in the basket. The princess said that he was one of the Israelites' children.

Miriam went to get her mother. The princess asked Miriam's mother to take care of the baby for her. When the baby got older, he went to live with Pharaoh's daughter. The princess named him Moses.

Moses grew up in the palace of the king of Egypt. He had the best of everything. God was preparing Moses. God was getting him ready to be a great leader.

The Talking Step

How does your family help you? How can you help your family?
  What are you learning now that will help when you are an adult?

🤲 The Praying Step

Dear God, thank You for giving me a good home and family. Help me to appreciate them more.

> My child, obey the teachings of your parents.
>
> *—Proverbs 1:8*

God Protected Moses from His Enemies

Exodus 2:11–25

 The Thinking Step

Have you ever been afraid that someone would try to hurt you?
What did you do about it?

The Listening Step

When Moses was a baby, God kept him safe in a basket on the river. He let Moses grow up as the son to the Egyptian king's daughter. But Moses knew he was an Israelite. He was one of God's people.

The Israelites were the slaves of the Egyptians. One day Moses saw an Egyptian hit an Israelite. Moses got so mad that he killed the Egyptian.

Moses did not think anyone saw him do that. But he was wrong. Soon the king of Egypt heard what Moses had done. He wanted to kill Moses, so Moses ran for his life.

Moses ran to the land of Midian. He sat down at a well to rest. There he helped some women take care of their father's sheep.

Moses began working with the women's father, Jethro. He even married Jethro's daughter, Zipporah. God watched over Moses. He kept him safe–again.

The Talking Step

Has God ever protected you from someone who tried to hurt you?
What happened?

✋ The Praying Step

Dear God, help me to know that You will always take care of me. Help me to trust You more.

> I trust you, LORD, and I claim you as my God.
>
> —*Psalm 31:14*

God Freed the Israelites from Egypt

Exodus 3:1–12:51

The Thinking Step

Have you ever thought God did not answer your prayers? Why?
Have you ever thought God did not hear your prayers? Why?

The Listening Step

The Israelites were God's people. God had promised them that they would live in a great land. But they were not in a great land. They were slaves in Egypt. They cried out to God. And God heard them.

God told Moses, "Go to the King! I am sending you to lead my people out of his country."

So Moses went to speak to Pharaoh: "The LORD God says 'Let my people go!'"

But Pharaoh did not believe Moses. So God proved to Pharaoh that he should let the Israelites go. Many things happened as signs from God. Water became blood. Cattle died. Darkness covered the earth. Finally, after ten signs, Pharaoh believed Moses. He let the people of Israel go.

God did not forget the Israelites. He answered their prayers. They finally left Egypt.

The Talking Step

Has God ever answered a prayer after you prayed it for a long time?
Did you feel like giving up on God? Why or why not?

🤚 The Praying Step

Dear God, I know You always hear me when I pray. Help me to remember that. Help me always to have faith in You.

> Never give up praying. And when you pray, keep alert and be thankful.
>
> *—Colossians 4:2*

God Saved the Israelites from the Red Sea

Exodus 13:17–14:31

 The Thinking Step

When was the last time you had a problem you could not solve? What was the problem? What did you do about it?

The Listening Step

God's people, the Israelites, were slaves in Egypt. God sent Moses to convince Pharaoh, the king of Egypt, to set the Israelites free.

Then Pharaoh changed his mind. He and other Egyptians did not want all their slaves to leave. So they chased after them. Soon the Israelites were trapped. The Red Sea was in front of them. And the Egyptians were behind them. They were scared.

"We had rather be slaves in Egypt than die in this desert!" they said to Moses. "Don't be afraid!" Moses said. "Be brave, and you will see the LORD save you today."

Moses held up his rod. The Red Sea divided. The Israelites walked right through the middle of the sea and away from the Egyptians! God had taken care of them again.

The Talking Step

Describe a time God solved a problem for you. Did you thank God?

🖐 The Praying Step

Dear God, I know nothing is too hard for You. Help me always to trust You. Thank You for watching over me and taking care of all my problems.

The LORD will fight for you, and you won't have to do a thing.

—Exodus 14:14

God Led the Israelites Through the Wilderness

Exodus 15:22–27

 The Thinking Step

Can you think of a time when things went from bad to worse? What happened? How did you feel about it? What did you do?

The Listening Step

God took good care of the Israelites. They could count on God to watch over them. He freed them from slavery in Egypt. And He led them safely through the Red Sea.

Then they had problems again. There was no water in the wilderness. They looked and looked. But there was nothing to drink. Soon the people of Israel came to Marah. There was water in Marah. But the water was too bitter to drink.

The people became upset. "What are we going to drink?" they complained to Moses.

God showed Moses a tree. Moses threw the tree in the water. The water became good to drink.

Next the people of Israel came to Elim. In Elim there were 12 wells of water and 70 palm trees. The Israelites had plenty to drink! They set up camp by the water. God took care of them. All they needed to do was follow Him.

The Talking Step

Can you think of a time you were happier after a problem than before it? Why? What happened?

✋ The Praying Step

Dear God, sometimes I go through hard times and problems. But I know You are still watching over me. Thank You for using problems to help me. Help me always to trust You.

> Let the LORD lead you and trust him to help.
>
> —*Psalm 37:5*

God Gave the Israelites Food

Exodus 16:1–36

🔢 The Thinking Step

Do you ever complain about things?
Does it work? Do people like to hear you complain?

👂 The Listening Step

God had prepared a special land for the Israelites. But they were in the wilderness. It had been more than a month since they left Egypt.

The people were hungry. So they complained again. "You have brought us out here into this desert, where we are going to starve," they said to Moses.

"The LORD has heard your complaints," Moses told the people. "You will know it is the LORD when he gives you meat each evening and more than enough bread each morning."

The next morning thin flakes were on the ground. "What is it?" the people asked Moses. "This is the bread that the LORD has given you to eat," Moses said. And he told them to gather what they needed.

The people collected all the bread they could. No one was hungry. God had taken care of them again, just as He promised.

🗣️ The Talking Step

Have you ever complained to God? Why? Why not?
What did you say? Did He answer you?

👋 The Praying Step

Dear God, I know You know what I am going through. Sometimes I do not like what is happening to me. I do not want to be a complainer. Help me to trust You more.

Because you belong to Christ Jesus, God will bless you with peace that no one can completely understand. And this peace will control the way you think and feel.

–Philippians 4:7

God Showed Moses the Promised Land

Deuteronomy 34:1–4

The Thinking Step

Did you ever want to see something or someone very much? What or who was it?

How did you feel when you saw that thing or person? Why?

The Listening Step

God promised Abraham that his great-grandchildren would live in a special land. Moses would lead the people of Israel to the land.

The Israelites had spent many years traveling in the wilderness. It was time to enter the land. But Moses would not lead them into the land. Joshua would do that.

Before Moses died, God took him to the top of a high mountain. Moses saw the Promised Land. He saw the cities and he saw the seas. He saw the plains and he saw the mountains.

"This is the land I was talking about when I solemnly promised Abraham, Isaac, and Jacob," God said to Moses. "I have let you see it."

Then Moses could die. God had taken good care of him. He even let him see the Promised Land.

The Talking Step

When was the last time God gave you something you really wanted? What was it?

Why do you think God gave it to you?

48

🖐 The Praying Step

Dear God, I do not always thank You for the little things You give me. Thank You for making me happy. Thank You for things that bring joy into my life.

> Do what the LORD wants, and he will give you your heart's desire.
>
> —*Psalm 37:4*

God Hid the Two Spies
from Danger

Joshua 2:1–24

The Thinking Step

When was the last time you hid from someone? Why?
What would have happened if the person had found you?

The Listening Step

Joshua was the new leader of the people of Israel. It was almost time for the Israelites to go into their new homeland. The first city in their path was Jericho. Jericho had a big wall around it.

Joshua sent two spies to look at the land. They came to the house of Rahab. She lived in Jericho. The king of Jericho found out that the spies were with Rahab.

The king's soldiers said to Rahab, "Let us have the men who are staying at your house. They are spies." But Rahab had hidden the spies on the roof of her house. "They left about sunset. I don't know where they were going, but if you hurry, maybe you can catch them," she said to the soldiers.

The two Israelites were safe. God would give them their new land.

The Talking Step

Describe a time God kept you safe.
What happened? How did God protect you?

✋ The Praying Step

Dear God, I know You watch over me. Thank You for keeping me safe.

> Protect me as you would your very own eyes; hide me in the shadow of your wings.
>
> —*Psalm 17:8*

God Protected Rahab

Joshua 2:8–21; 6:1–25

 ## The Thinking Step

When have your friends told you to do the wrong thing? What happened?

If you had to choose between obeying God and following your friends, which would you choose? Why?

The Listening Step

Rahab had heard about the Israelites. She knew God was taking care of them. She knew the Israelites would soon take the city she was living in.

One day two Israelite spies came to Rahab's house. When the king of her city heard about the men, he sent soldiers to arrest the spies. They demanded that Rahab let them have the men.

What should Rahab do? She had to decide whether to follow her friends or God. Rahab decided to hide the men. She knew they were from God. Rahab chose God's side.

Later, the Israelites took over Jericho, Rahab's city. But they did not forget Rahab. They protected Rahab and her family.

Rahab was saved. She chose to obey God rather than follow her friends. God protected her. Rahab had new friends, the Israelites. They believed in God, just as Rahab did.

The Talking Step

What happens when you follow your friends and disobey God?

How can you obey God and follow your friends at the same time?

✋ The Praying Step

Dear God, I want to obey You all the time. Help me to obey You even when others do not obey You. Give me friends who want to obey You, too.

You cannot be the slave of two masters! You will like one more than the other or be more loyal to one than the other. You cannot serve both God and money.
                                                    —*Matthew 6:24*

God Did the Impossible
for the Israelites

Joshua 6:1–27

The Thinking Step

Name something impossible.
  What makes it impossible?

The Listening Step

God promised the people of Israel a special land. It was time for them to move into that land. But people were already living there. One city, Jericho, even had a large wall around it.

God told Joshua that the Israelites would take over Jericho with His help. God told the people of Israel to march around Jericho once a day for six days. Then, on the seventh day, the Israelites got up early in the morning. That day they marched around Jericho seven times.

On the last march around the wall, Joshua said to the people of Israel, "Get ready to shout! The LORD will let you capture this town." Everyone shouted. Then the wall of Jericho fell to the ground. The Israelites obeyed God. And God did the impossible!

The Talking Step

Name a time God did the impossible.
  What did He do? Why was it impossible?

🖐 The Praying Step

Dear God, I know You can do the impossible. Help me to trust You to do the impossible in my life. Help me to obey You and to allow You to take care of me.

> Nothing is impossible for God!
>
> *–Luke 1:37*

God Stopped the Clock for the Israelites

Joshua 10:1–15

The Thinking Step

When did you wish a day would not end?
   Do you think that could ever happen? How?

The Listening Step

God helped the Israelites take over the city of Jericho. The king of Jerusalem saw how God took care of the Israelites. He was scared. He sent a message to some of the other kings. "Come and help me," he said.

They did. The armies from five cities got together to fight against the Israelites. But God took care of the Israelites again.

"Don't be afraid," God told Joshua. "I will help you defeat them." The Israelites surprised the armies. They ran for their lives. The Israelites could not catch everyone.

Joshua asked God for help. God made the sun and the moon stand still. It stayed daylight for an extra day. God also sent large hailstones in the path of those who were running from the Israelites and struck them down. God took care of the Israelites' problems.

The Talking Step

When has God given you more time in a day?
   What happened?

✋ The Praying Step

Dear God, I know You can do anything. Give me the time to do what You want me to do. Help me to use that time wisely.

This day belongs to the LORD!

—Psalm 118:24

God Gave Gideon a Sign

Judges 6:1–40

The Thinking Step

Has God ever spoken to you?
   What did He say?
   How did you know it was God?

The Listening Step

The people of Israel were in the land God had given them. It was a beautiful land. But people from Midian had taken over their land. The Israelites were very sad.

They cried out to God and God heard them. He spoke to Gideon, "I am giving you the power to rescue Israel from the Midianites."

But Gideon had to be sure God was really sending him. He put a piece of wool on the floor. "If you really will help me rescue Israel, then tomorrow morning let there be dew on the wool, but let the stone floor be dry," Gideon told God.

He woke up early the next morning. The floor was dry. But the wool was dripping wet! Gideon was still not convinced.

"Don't be angry at me," he said to God. "Let the wool be dry and the stone floor be wet with dew." The next morning that was exactly what happened. Gideon knew God would take care of him and the Israelites.

The Talking Step

How do you know when God wants you to do something?
   How do you know when God is speaking to you?

✋ The Praying Step

Dear God, please help me to listen to You. Show me when You are speaking to me. Help me always to do what You tell me.

Your teachings are sweeter than honey.

—Psalm 119:103

God Gave the Israelites Victory

Judges 7:1–25

？ The Thinking Step

Can you think of a time when your team had fewer players than the other team and still won?

What happened? Why were you able to win?

👂 The Listening Step

Gideon gathered his men together to fight the Midianites. "Your army is too big," God told Gideon. "The Israelites would think that they had won the battle all by themselves." God wanted the Israelites to know that He was saving them.

Gideon told everyone who was scared to go home, and 22,000 men went home. There were 10,000 men left. God told Gideon that was still too many.

Gideon told everyone to go down by the river. He watched how each man took a drink from the river. Most of the men got down on their knees to drink. Only 300 men cupped water in their hands and lapped it.

The 300 men defeated all the armies of Midian. God gave the land back to the Israelites.

🔊 The Talking Step

Would you rather be on a small team with God to help you or a big team without God's help? Why? Which team would win?

How can you make sure you're on God's team?

60

🤚 The Praying Step

Dear God, I want to be on Your team. I know sometimes we will be outnumbered by others. But as long as You are helping me, we will never lose.

> Thank God for letting our Lord Jesus Christ give us the victory!
>
> —*1 Corinthians 15:57*

God Gave Ruth a Family

Ruth 1–4

 ## The Thinking Step

Have you ever had to do something hard? What was it?
Why was it hard?

The Listening Step

Ruth lived in Moab. One day Ruth met a man from Judah. His father had died. He and his brother lived with their mother, Naomi. Soon he and Ruth got married. His brother married Orpah. Orpah was from Moab, too.

Both couples were married about ten years. Then both brothers died. Orpah and Ruth were alone again.

"Don't you want to go back home to your own mothers?" Naomi asked Ruth and Orpah. Orpah and Ruth cried. They did not want to return home. Finally Orpah left. But Ruth would not leave.

So Ruth returned with Naomi to her home in Judah. Soon Ruth met another man, Boaz. Boaz and Ruth were married. They had a son, Obed. Later Obed had a son, Jesse. And Jesse had a son, David. David became king of Israel. Ruth's great-grandson was David, king of Israel.

Ruth did something hard, and God took good care of her.

 ## The Talking Step

Name a time God told you to do something hard. Did He help you do it?
What happened? Did it lead to something better? How?

The Praying Step

Dear God, help me to always obey You even when You ask me to do hard things. I know even then You will take care of me.

Those who trust the LORD will find new strength. They will be strong like eagles soaring upward on wings; they will walk and run without getting tired.

—Isaiah 40:31

God Gave Hannah
What She Wanted

1 Samuel 1:1–20

The Thinking Step

When was the last time you were really unhappy? Why?
Do you think your sadness made God sad?

The Listening Step

Hannah was sad. She did not have any children.

One day Hannah went to the temple. She was so upset that she cried. "LORD," Hannah prayed, "please let me have a son. I will give him to you for as long as he lives." Hannah was so upset that her mouth was moving, but no words were coming out. Have you ever been that upset?

Eli, the priest, saw Hannah and won-dered what was wrong with her. "I do feel miserable and terribly upset," Hannah explained to Eli. "I've been telling the LORD about my problems."

"Go home now," Eli told Hannah. "I'm sure the God of Israel will answer your prayer." Hannah went home. Soon she was the mother of a baby boy. Hannah named her baby Samuel, which means "heard of God." Hannah prayed to God, and God answered her prayer.

The Talking Step

Have you ever told God that you were unhappy? Try it next time you are unhappy.
Do you think God could help you be happy?

🖐 The Praying Step

Dear God, sometimes I am unhappy because of what is happening to me. Help me to always follow You. Help me remember that You are always there to take care of me.

> Ask and you will receive, search and you will find, knock and the door will be opened for you.
>
> *—Luke 11:9*

God Gave Samuel a Good Teacher

1 Samuel 1:19–2:26

The Thinking Step

Who is your teacher? In school? In Sunday school?

How does your teacher help you?

The Listening Step

Samuel was a gift from God. His mother, Hannah, had asked God for a child. Samuel was the child God gave her. When Samuel was a few years old, his mother took him to Eli, the priest.

Hannah told Eli, "A few years ago I stood here beside you and asked the LORD to give me a child. Here he is! The LORD gave me just what I asked for. Now I am giving him to the LORD for as long as he lives."

Samuel's mother left him with Eli. Samuel did what Eli told him. Samuel served God. Eli taught Samuel the Bible. Eli taught Samuel about God.

Eli taught Samuel well. Samuel became a great prophet. God gave Samuel a good teacher.

The Talking Step

Why did God give you teachers?

How can your teachers help you serve God?

How can you learn more from your teachers?

🙏 The Praying Step

Dear God, thank You for giving me such good teachers. Help me to learn all I can from my teachers. I want to learn how to serve You.

Listen to instruction and do your best to learn.

—*Proverbs 23:12*

God Chose David

1 Samuel 16:1–13

⁇ The Thinking Step

Have you ever had a friend choose you? How did it make you feel? Why? When have you had to choose just one friend? How did you decide?

👂 The Listening Step

Israel needed a new king. "Go visit a man named Jesse," God told Samuel. "I've chosen one of his sons to be my king."

Jesse had many sons. Samuel did not know which son God had chosen. Samuel thought God had chosen Jesse's oldest son, Eliab. But he was wrong. God told Samuel, "People judge others by what they look like, but I judge people by what is in their hearts."

Samuel saw seven of Jesse's sons. But God did not choose any of them. "Do you have any more sons?" Samuel asked Jesse. "My youngest son, David, is out taking care of the sheep," said Jesse. "Send for him!" Samuel said.

God told Samuel that David was the one chosen to become king. Samuel had to go through David's seven brothers before he got to David. But David was the one God had chosen. God has chosen you, too.

🔊 The Talking Step

What does it mean that God chose you to be one of His children?
   How does it make you feel? Why?
   How does knowing God has chosen you help you when you have problems?

📖 The Praying Step

Dear God, thank You for choosing me. Help me always to remember that You chose me to be one of Your children.

> You are God's chosen and special people.
>
> *—1 Peter 2:9*

God Saved David from the Giant

1 Samuel 17

The Thinking Step

Have you ever faced a problem that you thought was too hard to solve? What was it? What happened?

The Listening Step

David had a giant problem named Goliath. He was over nine feet tall!

"I challenge Israel's whole army!" Goliath yelled. "Choose someone to fight me!" All the soldiers were scared of him.

David was not scared. "He's making fun of the army of the living God!" David said. "I'll go out and fight him myself!" He knew the Lord would keep him safe.

So David went out to fight Goliath. But first he stopped at the brook to pick up five smooth stones.

"You've come out to fight me with a sword," David called to Goliath, "but I've come out to fight you in the name of the LORD All-Powerful."

Then David pulled out a stone and put it in his slingshot. He slung the stone at Goliath. It hit him right in the forehead. Goliath fell down–dead! God took care of David and all the Israelites.

The Talking Step

Can God do anything? Can He solve any problem?

What should you do next time you have a very difficult problem? Why?

The Praying Step

Dear God, thank You for always taking care of me even when things look difficult. Help me always to trust You, just like David did.

There are some things that people cannot do, but God can do anything.

—*Mark 10:27*

God Saved David from King Saul

1 Samuel 24:1–22

✦ The Thinking Step

Are you a patient person? When has God not answered your prayers fast enough?

Have you ever tried solving a problem on your own instead of waiting for God to solve it? What happened?

✦ The Listening Step

God had promised that David would be the next king. But Saul was the current king. Saul did not like David. He did not like all the attention David got for killing Goliath.

One day King Saul heard that David was out in the wilderness. He took 3,000 men with him. He wanted to kill David. But God kept David safe.

King Saul found a cave near the road. He went inside. Saul did not know that David was also in that cave. David's men wanted to kill Saul. But David would not do that. Saul had been chosen by God to be king of Israel. If David fought against Saul, he would be fighting against God! So David only cut part of Saul's robe.

David let God protect him. He did not try to solve his problem by himself. Later David became the king of Israel.

The Talking Step

Does God need your help? Why? Why not?

Will God solve our problems if we let Him?

What might happen if we try to solve problems God should solve?

🖐 The Praying Step

Dear God, thank You for keeping me safe. Help me to let You take care of me. Help me to trust You more.

> The one who chose you can be trusted, and he will do this.
> —*1 Thessalonians 5:24*

God Helped Solomon to Be a Good King

1 Kings 3:1–15

 The Thinking Step

Have you ever been asked to do something that was too difficult for you to do?

What was it? Why was it so difficult? How did you do?

The Listening Step

David had been a good king. God was very happy with King David. But David's son, Solomon, had become king. He loved God, too. He wanted to be a good king just like King David.

One night God appeared to King Solomon in a dream. God promised to give him anything he wanted. "You've made me king," Solomon said, "but I'm very young. Please make me wise and teach me the difference between right and wrong." Solomon could have asked for anything. He could have asked God to be a rich man. But Solomon asked God for understanding to help others. That made God very happy.

God did what Solomon asked. God gave him more, too. He told Solomon, "You'll be rich and respected as long as you live."

God took care of Solomon. He made Solomon a good and wise king.

The Talking Step

Can you name a time when God helped you do something difficult?

Did you thank Him?

Think of something right now you could ask God to help you do.

74

🖐 The Praying Step

Dear God, sometimes You ask me to do things that are very hard. Many times I am not sure that I can do what You ask. Help me to do what You ask. Give me the strength to trust You.

Christ gives me the strength to face anything.

–Philippians 4:13

God Sent the Ravens to Feed Elijah

1 Kings 17:1–6

 The Thinking Step

When have you been really hungry? What happened?
Who took care of you?

 The Listening Step

Elijah was a prophet of God. He told people to obey God. Many times people disobeyed God anyway. Then Elijah had to tell them that God was going to punish them for disobeying Him. People did not like to hear that.

King Ahab was a very bad king. He did not think he had to obey God. One day Elijah went to see King Ahab.

"I'm a servant of the living LORD," he said. "It won't rain until I say so." The land became very dry. There was no food for anyone to eat.

God told Elijah to go to a brook. The ravens would feed him there. So that was what Elijah did. In the morning the ravens fed him. And in the evening the ravens fed him. God took good care of Elijah. He could even get a drink of water from the brook when he was thirsty.

 **The Talking Step**

Describe a time when God helped feed someone who was hungry.
How did God do it? Why do you think God would help feed a hungry person?
Why do you pray before you eat? How does God give you the food you eat?

76

🤚 The Praying Step

Thank You for taking care of us, God. Thank You for giving us our food each day.

Everyone depends on you, and when the time is right, you provide them with food.

—*Psalm 145:15*

God Saved the
Widow's Children

2 Kings 4:1–7

🔤 The Thinking Step

What is the most money you ever had?
  What would you do if you did not have any money?

🔤 The Listening Step

The woman was scared. Her husband had loved God. But he was dead. The woman did not have any money. And she and her husband owed a lot of money. A man was going to take her sons as slaves to pay back what she owed. The woman asked Elisha, the prophet, to help her.

"What do you have in your house?" Elisha asked her. "Nothing but a small bottle of olive oil," the woman told Elisha. "Ask your neighbors for their empty jars," Elisha told her. "Go home. Then begin filling the jars with oil."

The woman and her sons borrowed many jars. Then she poured oil into each one. "Sell the oil and use part of the money to pay what you owe," Elisha told the woman. "You and your sons can live on what is left."

God provided a miracle just when the woman needed it. He took care of her.

🔤 The Talking Step

Name a time when God took care of someone's need. What happened?
  Can God help you when you need help? Why?
  What should you do when you have a big need?

The Praying Step

Dear God, thank You for taking care of all my needs. Help me to trust You more. I know You will always take care of me.

I pray that God will take care of all your needs with the wonderful blessings that come from Christ Jesus!

—Philippians 4:19

God Kept the Israelites Safe While They Built the Walls

Nehemiah 4

The Thinking Step

Have you ever done the right thing and gotten in trouble? Why?

Have you ever obeyed God and had problems?

The Listening Step

Jerusalem was the city of God. The people of Israel loved Jerusalem. But when they disobeyed God, other nations destroyed Jerusalem.

Nehemiah wanted to rebuild the walls around Jerusalem. He told some of the people of Israel about his plans. They agreed to help.

But their enemies did not want the people of Israel to rebuild the walls. They started making fun of the Israelites.

"Look at the wall," one man yelled. "Why, even a fox could knock over this pile of stones."

But the wall kept going up. Nehemiah and the people asked God to give them strength. So Nehemiah set up men to keep guard day and night to protect those working on the wall.

The walls around Jerusalem were rebuilt. God kept the people safe. They were doing God's work.

The Talking Step

Do you think you would ever have problems if you were doing what God wanted? Why? Why not?

What should you do if you are doing what God wants and are having problems?

🖐 The Praying Step

Dear God, I want to do Your work. I want to do what You want me to do. Show me what You want. Help me not to lose faith in You. Keep watching over me.

> The LORD gives perfect peace to those whose faith is firm.
>
> —Isaiah 26:3

God Kept Jeremiah Safe

Jeremiah 36

The Thinking Step

Who are your best friends?

How do your friends help you?

Why did God give you friends?

The Listening Step

Jeremiah was a prophet. He lived at a sad time. Many people disobeyed God. God was going to punish them. God told Jeremiah to tell the people what was going to happen.

Jeremiah sent for his friend Baruch. Baruch wrote down what Jeremiah told him. Baruch then read the words in the house of the Lord. He also read them to the princes in the king's house.

"The king needs to hear this," they told Baruch. "You and Jeremiah must go into hiding, and don't tell anyone where you are."

The princes read to the king what Baruch had written. King Jehoiakim became so angry that he cut the scroll into pieces and threw them into the fire. Then King Jehoiakim told some men to arrest Baruch and Jeremiah. But they were hiding. Baruch was a good friend to Jeremiah. He did what Jeremiah asked him, and he helped protect Jeremiah. The princes helped Baruch and Jeremiah, too, by telling them to hide from the king. God gave Jeremiah helpful friends.

The Talking Step

Tell about a time God used one of your friends to help you.

Have you thanked God for your friends?

Have you asked God to give you good friends?

🖐 The Praying Step

Dear God, thank You for giving me good friends. Give me more good friends. Help me to know when to listen to my friends.

You are better off to do right, than to lose your way by doing wrong.

—*Proverbs 12:26*

83

God Protected Shadrach, Meshach, and Abednego

Daniel 3

The Thinking Step

Have you ever done anything because everyone was doing it? Why?

The Listening Step

King Nebuchadnezzar wanted everyone to worship the statue that he had made. But Shadrach, Meshach, and Abednego wanted to obey God.

Shadrach, Meshach, and Abednego were brought to King Nebuchadnezzar. The king told them that if they did not worship the statue, they would be thrown into a furnace. "We won't worship your gods and the gold statue you have set up," Shadrach, Meshach, and Abednego said. "The God we worship can save us from you and your flaming furnace."

King Nebuchadnezzar was furious. He commanded that the furnace be turned up seven times hotter than normal! Then Shadrach, Meshach, and Abednego were tied up and thrown into the furnace. When the king looked into the furnace, he was amazed. King Nebuchadnezzar shouted, "I see *four* men walking around in the fire. None of them is harmed, and the fourth one looks like a god."

Shadrach, Meshach, and Abednego went against everyone, even the king. And God kept them safe.

The Talking Step

Have you ever disobeyed God when you wanted to obey Him? Why?
What made you disobey God?
Would you obey God when everyone else was disobeying Him? Why? Why not?

84

The Praying Step

Dear God, sometimes it is hard to obey You when everyone else is disobeying You. Help me always to obey You. Help me to always remember that You will protect me when I obey Your commands.

> The LORD protects everyone who follows him, but the wicked follow a road that leads to ruin.
>
> —*Psalm 1:6*

God Shut the Mouths
of the Lions

Daniel 6:1–24

The Thinking Step

When was the last time you were mad at someone? Why were you mad?
Did you try to get even? Why?

The Listening Step

King Darius wanted to put Daniel in charge of his entire kingdom. But the king's other leaders did not like that. They told the king to make a new rule: anyone who prays to any god or man except you will be thrown into the lions' den. These men knew that Daniel prayed to God every day. They wanted to get Daniel in trouble.

Daniel kept praying. So the king had to put Daniel in the lions' den. Early the next morning the king went to see him. "Was your God able to save you from the lions?" King Darius called out. "My God sent an angel to keep the lions from eating me," Daniel answered.

The king was thrilled! He commanded that Daniel be taken out of the lions' den. Then the king commanded that the men who had tried to hurt Daniel be put in the lions' den. God took care of Daniel. And He punished Daniel's enemies, too.

The Talking Step

Should we try to get even with people who are mean, or should we let God punish evildoers? Why?

Describe a time you wanted to hurt someone who was mean to you but God took care of the problem.

The Praying Step

Dear God, sometimes I get angry when people are mean to me. I want to get even with them. Help me remember that You will punish those who do wrong. I want to leave it in Your hands.

Don't try to get even. Let God take revenge. In the Scriptures the Lord says, "I am the one to take revenge and pay them back."

—*Romans 12:19*

God Sent a Big Fish to Save Jonah

Jonah 1–2

? The Thinking Step

Have you ever done something that caused trouble for you and other people?

What happened?

The Listening Step

Jonah was a prophet. He spoke messages from God. One day God told Jonah to go to Nineveh. But Jonah did not want to go to Nineveh. He did not like the people there.

Instead of taking a ship to Nineveh, Jonah took a ship to Tarshish. Soon a big storm started rocking the ship. The men on the ship were scared. Jonah knew what caused the storm. He had disobeyed God.

"What should we do with you to make the sea calm down?" the men asked Jonah. Jonah knew what to do. "Throw me into the sea," he told them. So the men threw Jonah into the sea. But Jonah did not drown. God provided a big fish to swallow him. Jonah disobeyed God. But God took care of Jonah. He had a fish swallow Jonah and keep him safe.

The Talking Step

When has God taken care of you when you had a problem?

Do you think God would take care of you if you caused a problem by disobeying Him? Why? Why not?

🤚 The Praying Step

Dear God, thank You for always taking care of me, even when I cause my problems. Thank You for always being there to catch me when I fall.

The LORD will hold your hand, and if you stumble, you still won't fall.

—*Psalm 37:24*

God Gave Elizabeth a Son

Luke 1:5–25

The Thinking Step

When have you gotten a reward or privilege because you obeyed?
    Does your class at school get special privileges if everyone is good? Why?

The Listening Step

Elizabeth and her husband, Zechariah, had always obeyed God. But they did not have any children. That made them very sad.

One day an angel appeared to Zechariah. The angel scared him. "Don't be afraid, Zechariah!" the angel said. "Your wife Elizabeth will have a son, and you must name him John." But Zechariah did not believe the angel. Because of that, Zechariah was not able to speak until the baby was born. Elizabeth believed she would have her baby boy. She named him John.

Elizabeth's baby had an important job. His job was to tell people that Jesus was coming. He helped people get ready to meet Jesus. Elizabeth's baby became John the Baptist.

Elizabeth believed God. She obeyed God. And God gave her something wonderful–a baby.

The Talking Step

Do you obey God? Why?
    Do you think God rewards people who obey Him? Why? How?

🖐 The Praying Step

Dear God, help me to obey You. I want to be the kind of person that You want to reward. I want to be a good child of Yours.

A crown will be given to me for pleasing the Lord. He judges fairly, and on the day of judgment he will give a crown to me and to everyone else who wants him to appear with power.

—2 Timothy 4:8

God Made Mary Special

Luke 1:26–38

The Thinking Step

Have you ever missed out on some fun because you were not willing to do something?

What was it? What was it that you were not willing to do?

The Listening Step

Mary was very happy. She was about to be married. She had a long life of exciting things ahead of her. Then one night an angel appeared to Mary. And her life changed forever.

"Don't be afraid!" the angel said to her. "God is pleased with you, and you will have a son. His name will be Jesus."

Mary loved God. If God wanted her to give birth to God's Son, she was willing!

Mary turned to the angel. "I am the Lord's servant!" she said. "Let it happen as you have said."

Mary was willing to be used by God. She would be special forever.

The Talking Step

Would you be willing to do what God asked? Why? Why not?

If He asked you to do something that did not make sense, would you do it? Why? Why not?

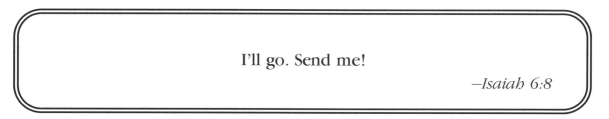 The Praying Step

Dear God, I want to serve You. I am willing to do what You want me to do.

> I'll go. Send me!
>
> —*Isaiah 6:8*

God Gave the Shepherds the Message First

Luke 2:8–20

The Thinking Step

Do you feel unimportant sometimes? Why?
What would make you feel more important?

The Listening Step

Nobody paid much attention to the shepherds. They just watched the sheep. But they were important to God.

When Jesus was born, angels were sent to announce His birth. Who do you think they announced the message to first? The shepherds.

At first the shepherds were afraid. But an angel said to them, "Don't be afraid! I have good news for you, which will make everyone happy. This very day in King David's hometown a Savior was born for you. He is Christ the Lord."

The shepherds then went to see Jesus. He was lying in a manger. After the shepherds saw Jesus, they told everyone what the angel had told them. The shepherds spread the message about Jesus. They were important after all.

The Talking Step

Do you think you are important to God? Why? Why not?
Do you think one person is more important than someone else in God's eyes?

🤚 The Praying Step

Dear God, sometimes I do not feel important. Help me always to remember that I am important to You.

> Think how much the Father loves us. He loves us so much that he lets us be called his children, as we truly are.
>
> —1 John 3:1

Jesus Forgave and Healed the Paralyzed Man

Matthew 9:1–8; Mark 2:1–12; Luke 5:17–26

The Thinking Step

Can people know what you are thinking if you do not tell them?

Do they know what you are going to say before you say it? How do they know that?

The Listening Step

Jesus was very popular. Many people wanted to see Him. One day Jesus was teaching in a house. Four men came to the house carrying a man lying on a mat. The man was paralyzed. His friends wanted Jesus to heal him. But so many people were there that the men could not get into the house to see Jesus. So they climbed up to the roof. Then the men made a hole in the roof and lowered the man to Jesus.

"My friend, your sins are forgiven," Jesus said to him. "Pick up your mat and walk home."

The man got up, picked up his mat, and walked out! Jesus knew the man wanted to be healed. But He also knew the man needed to have his sins forgiven. Jesus knew what the man needed, even more than he did!

The Talking Step

Do you think God knows what you need better than you do? Why?

Do you think God knows what you want before you ask Him? Why?

✋ The Praying Step

Dear God, thank You for watching over me. Thank You for knowing what I need before I ask You.

> Your Father knows what you need before you ask.
>
> —*Matthew 6:8*

Jesus Brought Jairus's Daughter Back to Life

Matthew 9:18–26; Mark 5:21–43; Luke 8:40–56

The Thinking Step

Is it ever too late to solve a problem?

Name a time you waited until the last possible moment to ask your parents for help. Did they help you?

The Listening Step

A leader of the synagogue, Jairus, came to see Jesus one day. "My daughter is about to die!" he told Jesus. "Please come and touch her, so she will get well and live." "Don't worry," Jesus told him. "Just have faith."

When Jesus arrived at the house, everyone was crying. The girl had just died. She was only 12 years old. "Why are you crying and carrying on like this?" Jesus said. "The child is not dead. She is just asleep."

Everyone laughed at Jesus. They did not understand what He meant.

Jesus told everyone to leave. Then He took the little girl by the hand and said, "Little girl, get up!" The girl opened her eyes and sat up. Jesus called her parents and told them to give her something to eat.

Jairus was glad that he asked Jesus to help him. He learned that it was not too late to ask Jesus for help.

The Talking Step

Is it ever too late to ask God for help? Why? Why not?

Why do you think we wait until the last possible moment to ask God to help us?

Why do we sometimes think it is too late to ask for God's help?

98

🤚 The Praying Step

Dear God, I am glad You want to help me. I know sometimes You are just waiting for me to ask You to help. Help me not to wait until the last moment to ask for Your help.

> Don't worry about anything, but pray about everything. With thankful hearts offer up your prayers and requests to God.
>
> *–Philippians 4:6*

Jesus Healed the Man with a Crippled Hand

Matthew 12:9–13; Mark 3:1–6; Luke 6:6–11

 The Thinking Step

Have you ever gotten in trouble for trying to help someone? What happened? How did it make you feel? Would you do it again? Why? Why not? Has anyone ever gotten in trouble for helping you? Why? How did you feel then?

The Listening Step

It was the Sabbath. The Sabbath was the Lord's Day. Jesus went into the synagogue. He taught the people about God.

Jesus saw a man in the synagogue who was hurt. His right hand was crippled. Some people did not think Jesus should help the man on the Sabbath. They thought the Sabbath should be used only for worshiping God.

"If you had a sheep that fell into a ditch on the Sabbath," Jesus asked them, "wouldn't you lift it out? People are worth much more than sheep, and so it is right to do good on the Sabbath."

Then Jesus turned to the man who was hurt. "Hold out your hand," Jesus said to him. The man stretched out his hand. When he did, it was healed.

The Talking Step

Would there ever be a time that God could not help you? Why? Why not? Do you think God wants to help you? Why? Why not?

The Praying Step

Dear God, thank You for always helping me. Thank You for never being too busy for me. I need Your help.

The LORD is your protector, and he won't go to sleep or let you stumble.

—*Psalm 121:3*

Jesus Healed the Army Officer's Servant from a Distance

Matthew 8:5–13; Luke 7:1–10

The Thinking Step

Do you know someone who tells other people what to do?
Do they do what he or she tells them? Why? Why not?

The Listening Step

Jesus had just entered Capernaum. An army officer, a Roman soldier, ran up to Him. "My servant is at home in such terrible pain that he can't even move," he told Jesus. "I will go and heal him," Jesus said.

But the officer did not want Jesus to come to his house. "I'm not good enough for you to come into my house," he told Jesus. "Just give the order, and my servant will get well."

The officer was very important in the Roman army. He had many people under his command. When he gave orders, people obeyed them. He knew Jesus was important, too. If Jesus said that his servant would be healed, he knew he would be healed.

Jesus was amazed: "I've never found anyone with this much faith!" Then Jesus turned to the officer. "You may go home now," He said. "Your faith has made it happen." When the officer got home, his servant was well.

The Talking Step

Can God do anything He wants? Is He in control of everything that happens?
How does this make you feel? Why?

🤲 The Praying Step

Dear God, I know You can do whatever You want. Thank You for always taking care of me. Help me to trust You more.

> Calm down, and learn that I am God! All nations on earth will honor me.
>
> —*Psalm 46:10*

Jesus Stopped the Funeral of the Widow's Son

Luke 7:11–17

The Thinking Step

What is the saddest thing you have ever seen?
Did you try to help? Why? Why not?

The Listening Step

Everywhere Jesus went He attracted a crowd. One day Jesus entered the city of Nain. His disciples were with Him. So were many other people.

A funeral procession was leaving the city. A young man had just died. He was the only son in his family. His father was already dead.

Jesus took one look at the mother. She had no one left. She was all alone. He felt sorry for her. "Don't cry," Jesus said to her.

Then Jesus walked over to the dead young man who was being carried out of the city to be buried. The men carrying him stopped. Jesus looked at the man lying there. "Young man," Jesus said, "get up!" The man sat up and started talking. Jesus gave him back to his mother.

The Talking Step

Do you think God is ever sad? Why?
What do you think He does about it?

The Praying Step

Dear God, thank You that You understand when I am sad. Thank You for helping me be happy.

He will wipe all tears from their eyes, and there will be no more death, suffering, crying, or pain. These things of the past are gone forever.

—*Revelation 21:4*

Jesus Encouraged John's Disciples

Matthew 11:2–6; Luke 7:18–23

 The Thinking Step

When was the last time you were discouraged?
What happened? What did you do about it?

The Listening Step

John the Baptist and Jesus were cousins. John the Baptist told people about Jesus. He even baptized Jesus. One day John the Baptist saw Jesus coming. "Here is the Lamb of God who takes away the sin of the world!" he told everyone.

But now John the Baptist was in prison. He had a lot of time to think. He had a lot of questions, too. So he sent two of his disciples to see Jesus. "Are you the one we should be looking for? Or must we wait for someone else?" they asked Jesus.

"Go and tell John what you have heard and seen," Jesus said to them. "The blind are now able to see, and the lame can walk. People with leprosy are being healed, and the deaf can hear. The dead are raised to life, and the poor are hearing the good news."

John the Baptist understood. He knew Jesus was the Messiah. Jesus helped him feel better.

The Talking Step

Who was the last person to encourage you? What did he or she do?
Does God ever encourage you? How?

🖐 The Praying Step

Dear God, sometimes I get discouraged. Thank You for encouraging me. I want to let You encourage me more. Next time I want to turn to You for help first.

> Two are better than one, because they have a good reward for their labor.
>
> *–Ecclesiastes 4:9*

Jesus Healed the Man Who Could Not Speak or See

Matthew 12:22–30; Luke 11:14–23

 The Thinking Step

Who is the strongest person you know?

> Could you defeat this person? Could you defeat this person if you had some help?
>
> Who could help you defeat this strong person?

 The Listening Step

Jesus loved everyone. He wanted to help people. One day some people brought a man to see Jesus. They wanted Jesus to help him. The man could not see or speak.

Jesus knew why the man could not see or speak. But Jesus is stronger than sickness, and He could help the man. Jesus healed him. The man could see. He could speak, too.

Everyone was shocked: "Could Jesus be the Son of David?"

The Pharisees were not convinced. "He forces out demons by the power of the ruler of the demons," they said.

Jesus explained that Satan would not defeat himself. Jesus took care of people even when Satan was hurting them.

 The Talking Step

Can anyone defeat God? Why not?

> What do you do when you are having problems? Why? What should you do?

108

✋ The Praying Step

Dear God, sometimes I have problems I cannot solve. You are the only One who can help me. Please help me solve my problems.

> You, LORD, are the light that keeps me safe. I am not afraid of anyone. You protect me, and I have no fears.
>
> –*Psalm 27:1*

Jesus Saved the Disciples

Matthew 8:23–27; Mark 4:36–41; Luke 8:22–25

 ## The Thinking Step

When was the first time you were really scared? Why?
Was there someone who could help you? Who?
Why did you think that person could help you?

The Listening Step

Jesus was very tired. He had been teaching people all day.

When it was night, Jesus said to the disciples, "Let's cross the lake."

They got in the boat, and Jesus found a pillow. Soon He was sound asleep. Then a storm came. The waves went higher and higher. The boat started filling up with water. The disciples got scared. They looked for Jesus. He was asleep in the back of the boat.

"Don't you care that we're about to drown?" they asked Him. Jesus got up. He shouted to the wind and waves to be still. The wind slowed down. The waves stopped. The disciples were amazed. They said, "Who is this? Even the winds and the waves obey Him!"

The disciples were scared, but Jesus took care of them. All they had to do was ask.

The Talking Step

Name someone you trust. Why do you trust that person?
Do you trust God? Why? How does that make you feel when you are scared?

The Praying Step

Dear God, I trust You. I know You will take care of me. Help me to put more faith in You. Help me to trust You more.

> Your way is perfect, LORD, and your word is correct. You are a shield for those who run to you for help.
>
> *—Psalm 18:30*

Jesus Responded to the Touch of the Sick Woman

Matthew 9:18–22; Mark 5:25–34; Luke 8:43–48

 The Thinking Step

Name a person you depend on.

Why do you depend on this person? Why do you trust him or her?

The Listening Step

People were excited to see Jesus. They had been waiting a long time. Crowds pressed all around Him.

A woman was there who had been sick for 12 years. She had spent all her money on doctor bills, but she was still sick. She wanted Jesus to heal her. "If I can just touch his clothes, I will get well," she said to herself.

The woman came up behind Jesus and touched His clothes. As soon as she touched them, she became well.

"Who touched me?" Jesus asked. Then He turned around and saw the woman. She knelt down before Jesus and explained why she touched Him. "Don't worry!" Jesus told her. "You are now well because of your faith."

She believed in Jesus, and He made her well.

The Talking Step

Name a time you trusted God to take care of you. What happened?

What is something you could trust God for today?

The Praying Step

Dear God, I have faith in You. I know You can take care of me. I want to trust You more.

> If you have faith when you pray, you will be given whatever you ask for.
>
> —*Matthew 21:22*

Jesus Helped Two Blind Men to See

Matthew 9:27–31

The Thinking Step

Do you know someone who can do anything? Who?
  Why do you think this person can do anything?

The Listening Step

Jesus had just helped a lot of people. He had healed a woman who had been sick for 12 years, and He had brought a little girl back to life. People wanted to be near Jesus. They wanted Him to teach them about God and heal them.

Two blind men called out to Jesus: "Have pity on us!" They wanted Jesus to help them see again. Jesus walked up to the two blind men: "Do you believe that I can make you well?" "Yes, Lord," they answered.

Jesus reached out His hands and touched their eyes. "Because of your faith, you will be healed," He said to them. As soon as Jesus said that, the men could see. They believed in Jesus, and He healed them.

The Talking Step

Do you believe God can help you? Why?
  What can you do to show God you believe in Him?

🖐 The Praying Step

Dear God, I believe in You. I want to show You I have faith in You. I want to allow You to take care of me.

Faith makes us sure of what we hope for and gives us proof of what we cannot see.

—*Hebrews 11:1*

Jesus Fed 5,000 Men

Matthew 14:13–21; Mark 6:32–44; Luke 9:10–17; John 6:1–13

 The Thinking Step

Have you ever been really hungry? How did you feel? What did you do?

The Listening Step

Jesus wanted to be alone. He took a boat across the lake to a place where no one lived. But the people followed Him.

When Jesus saw all the people, He felt sorry for them. Many of them were sick. Jesus healed them. Then He taught them about God.

Jesus' disciples said to Him, "Let the crowds leave, so they can go to the villages and buy some food."

"They don't have to leave," Jesus told them. "Why don't you give them something to eat?" "We have only five small loaves of bread and two fish," the disciples told Jesus.

The disciples brought the food to Jesus. Jesus took the food and blessed it. Then He gave it to the disciples to pass out to the people. All the people ate until they could not eat any more.

Jesus took care of the hungry people. He gave them food to eat. They were not hungry anymore.

The Talking Step

Do you think God cares when you are hungry? Why? Why not?

Do you think God gives you food to eat when you need it?

🤲 The Praying Step

Dear God, thank You for taking care of me. Thank You for making sure I have food to eat and keeping me from going hungry.

More than anything else, put God's work first and do what he wants. Then all the other things will be yours as well.

—Matthew 6:33

Jesus Let the Disciples Help Him

Matthew 10:1–11:1; Mark 6:7–13, 30; Luke 9:1–10

The Thinking Step

When was the last time you helped your mom or dad? Did they need your help?

Have your parents or teacher let you help them when they did not need your help? Why?

The Listening Step

Jesus called the disciples together. He had something to tell them. Jesus was sending the disciples out in groups of two. They were going to tell people about Jesus. They were even going to heal the sick people.

Jesus did not *need* the disciples' help. He *let* the disciples help Him. He wanted them to have the same joy of helping people that He had.

"As you go, preach, saying, 'The kingdom of heaven is at hand,'" Jesus told them.

The disciples had seen Jesus do these things. Now it was their turn. Jesus gave them the power to help people. Jesus lets us help people, too, just like the disciples.

The Talking Step

When was the last time you helped someone?

How did it make you feel? Why?

✋ The Praying Step

Dear God, thank You for letting me help people. Thank You for letting me serve You. I know You don't *need* my help. But I'm glad You let me help You.

> Serve the LORD with gladness.
>
> —*Psalm 100:2*

Jesus Saved Peter

Matthew 14:22–33; Mark 6:45–52; John 6:15–21

The Thinking Step

Have you ever been in real danger? What happened?
   What did you do to get saved?

The Listening Step

Jesus had helped people all day. It was late, so He sent the people home. Then He told the disciples to get in the boat and go to the other side of the lake. Jesus was finally alone.

Very early in the morning the winds started blowing. The waves blew the disciples back and forth in their boat. Jesus came out to see them, walking on the water! When the disciples saw Him, they were scared. They thought it was a ghost. "I am Jesus. Don't be afraid," Jesus called back.

Peter got out of the boat and started walking on the water toward Jesus. Then he looked around and saw the waves and the wind. He began to sink. "Lord, save me!" Peter yelled. Jesus held out His hand and pulled Peter out of the water. Jesus saved Peter. All Peter had to do was ask.

The Talking Step

What is the first thing you should do when you find yourself in danger? Why?
   Do you think God can help you? Why? How?

The Praying Step

Dear God, sometimes I see danger and get scared. Help me to ask You for help first.

Even when I am afraid, I keep on trusting you.

—Psalm 56:3

Jesus Healed the Gentile Woman's Daughter

Matthew 15:21–28; Mark 7:24–30

The Thinking Step

What do you do when you really want something?

Do you ask only once? Or do you keep asking until you get it? Why?

The Listening Step

One day Jesus went into a town and entered a house. He did not want anyone to know where He was. Jesus wanted to be alone.

A woman found out where Jesus was. She ran into the house and bowed down before Jesus. "Have pity on me!" she said. She told Him that her daughter was very sick.

"I was only sent to help the people of Israel!" Jesus told her. "It isn't right to take food away from children and feed it to the dogs."

"That's true," the woman told Him, "but even dogs get the crumbs that fall from their owner's table." "Dear woman," Jesus said, amazed, "you really do have a lot of faith, and you will be given what you want."

She got up and went home. Her daughter was well. The woman did not give up. And Jesus helped her.

The Talking Step

How many times do you ask God for something? Why?

Would you ever argue with God? Why? Why not?

✋ The Praying Step

Dear God, sometimes there are things I want. Help me to want what You know is best for me. I will not stop praying even when You do not seem to answer my prayers right away.

> Ask and you will receive, search and you will find, knock and the door will be opened for you.
>
> —*Luke 11:9*

Jesus Shared with Peter, James, and John

Matthew 17:1–13; Mark 9:2–8; Luke 9:28–36

The Thinking Step

Has someone ever showed you something important? What was it?
How did it make you feel? Why?

The Listening Step

One day Jesus, Peter, James, and John went up on a high mountain. Jesus' face started to shine like the sun. His clothes became bright white, too. Suddenly Moses and Elijah appeared and began talking with Jesus. The disciples were amazed.

Just as that was happening, a bright cloud came right over where they were standing. A voice came out of the cloud: "This is my own dear Son, and I am pleased with him."

Peter, James, and John were scared. They fell down on the ground.

"Get up," Jesus said. "Don't be afraid!"

"It is good for us to be here!" Peter said.

Peter, James, and John would remember that day the rest of their lives.

The Talking Step

Name a time God showed you something important. What was it? Why was it important?

Why do you think God shared it with you?

🙏 The Praying Step

Dear God, thank You for showing me special things. Thank You most of all for showing me Your love.

> The Word became a human being and lived here with us. We saw his true glory, the glory of the only Son of the Father. From him all the kindness and all the truth of God have come down to us.
>
> —John 1:14

Jesus Raised Lazarus from the Dead

John 11:1–44

The Thinking Step

Think of a time when something happened later than you wanted it to happen.

What did you do?

The Listening Step

One day Jesus heard that Lazarus was very sick. Jesus loved Lazarus very much. Everyone expected Jesus to go to Lazarus right away. But Jesus waited two more days before He went to see him. "His sickness will bring glory to God and his Son," Jesus said.

By the time Jesus went to see him, Lazarus had died. When Martha, Lazarus's sister, saw Jesus coming, she went out to meet Him. "Lord, if you had been here," she said, "my brother would not have died." "Your brother will live again!" Jesus told her.

They took Jesus to the cave where Lazarus was buried. "Lazarus, come out!" Jesus called. Lazarus, wrapped in grave-clothes, came out of the cave. He was alive! Many more people believed in Jesus. Lazarus died so people could see that Jesus was God's Son.

The Talking Step

What has God done that did not make any sense to you? Did you understand later why God did it?

Why do you think we do not always understand God's actions?

👐 The Praying Step

Dear God, I do not always understand why You do the things You do. But I know You always have a reason for everything You do. Help me to let You do things Your way.

> Just as the heavens are higher than the earth, my thoughts and my ways are higher than yours.
>
> —*Isaiah 55:9*

Jesus Healed Ten Men with Leprosy

Luke 17:11–19

The Thinking Step

Do you always thank people when they do nice things for you? Why?

Do you ever forget to say, "Thank you"? How do you think that makes people feel?

The Listening Step

People with leprosy were very sick. Other people did not want to be around them because they were afraid they might become sick, too. So the people with leprosy were forced to live apart from others.

Jesus was on His way to Jerusalem. One day He walked through a village. Some men with leprosy saw Him with His disciples.

"Jesus," they shouted, "have pity on us!" Jesus looked over at them. They were standing far away from Him.

"Go," Jesus said, "show yourselves to the priests." All ten men ran as fast as they could. As they went, they were healed.

When he saw that he was well again, one man stopped and ran back to Jesus. He thanked Jesus for healing him.

"Get up and go," Jesus told him. "Your faith has made you well."

Jesus was glad the man came back to thank Him.

The Talking Step

What was the last thing God did for you? Did you thank Him? If not, why not?

Think of one thing God has done that you have not thanked Him for. Thank Him for it today.

🤚 The Praying Step

Dear God, You do so many things to help me. Thank You for all You do for me. I love You.

Praise the LORD and pray in his name! Tell everyone what he has done.

—*Psalm 105:1*

Jesus Found Zacchaeus

Luke 19:1–10

 The Thinking Step

Have you ever been lost? What happened?
  Did someone find you? How?

The Listening Step

Zacchaeus wanted to see Jesus. But Zacchaeus had a problem. Many people were always with Jesus. And Zacchaeus was short. He could not see over all the people. Zacchaeus could not get close enough to see Jesus.

Zacchaeus had an idea. He ran ahead of the crowd and climbed a tree. He was higher than everyone. He could see Jesus! Jesus saw him, too.

"Zacchaeus, hurry down!" Jesus called to him. "I want to stay with you today."

Zacchaeus hurried down from the tree. Jesus wanted to stay at his house! "Today you and your family have been saved," Jesus said.

Jesus found Zacchaeus. And He saved him.

The Talking Step

How did Jesus find you?
  Do you know someone who did not believe in Jesus and then became a Christian?
  What did God do to help that person believe? Did He seek him or her out?

🤚 The Praying Step

Dear God, thank You for finding me. Please help lots of people I know come to know You.

> The Son of Man came to look for and to save people who are lost.
>
> —*Luke 19:10*

Jesus Praised Mary's Actions

Matthew 26:6–13; Mark 14:3–9; Luke 7:37–39; John 12:1–8

The Thinking Step

What is the nicest thing anyone ever did for you?
    Did you pay that person back? Why? How?

The Listening Step

Mary wanted to do something for Jesus. So she opened a bottle of expensive perfume and poured it on Jesus' feet. Then Mary wiped His feet dry with her hair. The smell of perfume filled the entire house.

Judas, one of Jesus' disciples, was upset. "Why such a waste? We could have sold this perfume and given the money to the poor!" he said.

"Leave her alone!" Jesus said. "She has done a beautiful thing for me. Wherever the good news is told all over the world, people will remember what she has done. And they will tell others."

Jesus made sure people would remember Mary.

The Talking Step

Has God ever paid you back for something you did for Him?
    What was it? How did God pay you back?

✋ The Praying Step

Dear God, I know I can never pay You back for what You have done for me. But I want to serve You.

> Do your work willingly, as though you were serving the Lord himself, and not just your earthly master. In fact, the Lord Christ is the one you are really serving, and you know that he will reward you.
>
> *–Colossians 3:23–24*

Jesus Cried Over Jerusalem

Matthew 23:37–39; Luke 13:34–35

 ## The Thinking Step

When was the last time you cried? Why did you cry?
What does it take to make you cry?

The Listening Step

Jesus was God's Son. He was there when most of the people of Israel followed God. Jesus was also there when many of the people of Israel disobeyed God.

The Israelites were God's chosen ones. Jerusalem was the capital city of Israel. It was the holy city.

Just before Jesus was to be crucified, He talked about the city of Jerusalem. Then He cried. Jesus thought of how much God loved the people.

"Jerusalem, Jerusalem!" Jesus cried. "I have often wanted to gather your people, as a hen gathers her chicks under her wings."

Jesus loved the people of Israel.

The Talking Step

Do you think you ever make Jesus cry? How?
What could you do to make Jesus stop crying?

134

🖐 The Praying Step

Dear God, please forgive me for the times I have made You sad. Help me to love You and obey You.

> So I confessed my sins and told them all to you. I said, "I'll tell the LORD each one of my sins." Then you forgave me and took away my guilt.
>
> —*Psalm 32:5*

Jesus Served the Disciples

John 13:1–20

🄿 The Thinking Step

Have you ever been served? Who served you? How did they serve you?
How did it make you feel?

🄰 The Listening Step

It was time for Jesus and the disciples to share the Passover meal. The meal had been prepared. The disciples and Jesus were going to share it together in the Upper Room.

It was the end of the day by the time Jesus and the disciples met together to eat. Their feet were dirty from being on the roads all day. Everyone's feet needed to be washed. Usually a servant did that. But that night was different.

Jesus got up from the table. Then He took off His outer clothes and put a towel around Himself. Jesus took a bowl and poured water into it. Jesus then walked up to Peter.

"Lord, are you going to wash my feet?" Peter asked Him.

"You don't really know what I am doing," Jesus said, "but later you will understand it."

Jesus was giving the disciples an example. Just as He served them, they were to serve each other.

🄰 The Talking Step

Did God ever serve you? How? What did He do?
Have you ever served others? How?

136

✋ The Praying Step

Dear God, thank You for serving me. Help me to serve You. Help me to serve others, too.

> The Son of Man did not come to be a slave master, but a slave who will give his life to rescue many people.
>
> —*Mark 10:45*

Jesus Prayed for the Disciples

John 17

The Thinking Step

Do you know someone who would do anything to help you? What would that person do?

How does that make you feel? Why?

The Listening Step

Jesus knew He would soon be arrested. Then He would be in a long trial. And the next day He would be crucified. Jesus did not want to die. But He knew that was what God wanted.

Jesus wanted to pray. But Jesus did not pray for Himself. He prayed for the disciples.

"I am praying for them," Jesus said.

"Father, keep them safe by the power of the name that you have given me. I don't ask you to take my followers out of the world, but keep them safe from the evil one."

Jesus had a lot on His mind. But He still prayed for us. He took care of us even at the end of His life on earth.

The Talking Step

Do you think Jesus is still watching over us?

What does He do to help us?

🖐 The Praying Step

Dear God, thank You for watching over me. Thank You for being concerned about everything in my life and for taking care of me.

> Even the hairs on your head are counted.
> —*Matthew 10:30*

Jesus Saved the World

Matthew 27:35–44; Mark 15:24–32; Luke 23:33–43; John 19:18–27

The Thinking Step

Have you ever been saved by someone? What did that person do for you?
Have you ever had someone sacrifice himself or herself to help you?

The Listening Step

Sin entered the world a long time ago. Everyone deserved to be punished. But God sent Jesus to be punished in our place.

Some people wanted Jesus to die. They took Him outside Jerusalem. They nailed Jesus to a cross and left Him there to die. Many people were there. They were all making fun of Jesus. "He saved others," they said, "but he can't save himself. If he is the Messiah, let him come down from the cross!" But Jesus just prayed for them.

"Father, forgive these people!" He said. "They don't know what they're doing."

One of the thieves dying with Jesus believed in Him. He turned to Jesus and said, "Remember me when you come into power!" "I promise that today you will be with me in paradise," Jesus said.

Then it was over. Jesus paid the punishment for everyone's sin. Jesus gave us all a way to heaven.

The Talking Step

What do you need to do to allow Jesus to save you? Have you done that?
Have you thanked Jesus for saving you?

140

🖐 The Praying Step

Dear God, thank You for sending Jesus to pay the punishment for me. Help me to always remember that You saved me.

> But God showed how much he loved us by having Christ die for us, even though we were sinful.
>
> —*Romans 5:8*

Jesus Rose Again

Matthew 28:1–7; Mark 16:1–7; Luke 24:1–12; John 20:1–9

 ## The Thinking Step

Have you ever been to a funeral? What happened?
 What would you think if the dead person became alive again?
 Do you think that could ever happen? Why? Why not?

The Listening Step

Jesus' disciples were sad. Jesus had died. Many people believed in Jesus. They were sad, too. What would everyone do without Him?

It was Sunday. Jesus had been dead two days. Mary, the sister of Lazarus, and Mary Magdalene went to the tomb where Jesus was buried. Suddenly there was a great earthquake. An angel came down from heaven and rolled the stone away from the tomb.

Mary and Mary Magdalene were scared. "Don't be afraid!" the angel said. He told them that Jesus was risen. And he added, "Go and tell his disciples."

The women became excited! Mary Magdalene told Peter and John first. Peter and John started running toward the tomb. They had to see for themselves. They believed, too. Jesus had defeated death. We can live with Him forever!

 ## The Talking Step

What would your life be like if Jesus had never risen from the dead? Why?
 Because Jesus rose from the dead, what can you learn about God's power?
 What can you learn about death?

🖐 The Praying Step

Dear God, thank You for defeating death. Thank You for giving me life. I want to spend it with You forever.

> Adam brought death to all of us, and Christ will bring life to all of us.
>
> *—1 Corinthians 15:22*

Jesus Forgave Peter

John 18:15–27; 21:1–24

⁉️ The Thinking Step

Have you ever asked someone to forgive you? What happened? What did the person say?

How did it make you feel?

👂 The Listening Step

Peter was sad. He had told Jesus he would never be ashamed of Him. But then Jesus was arrested. And Peter was asked if he knew Jesus. Three times Peter said that he never knew Jesus.

Jesus was alive again. And He and Peter were together. What do you think Jesus said to him?

Jesus asked Peter a question: "Do you love me?" "Yes, Lord," Peter answered, "you know I do!"

Then Jesus asked Peter again, "Do you love me?" "Yes, Lord, you know I love you!" Peter answered.

Jesus asked him a third time: "Do you love me?"

Peter was sad that Jesus had to ask him three times. "Lord, you know everything," Peter said. "You know I love you."

"Follow me!" Jesus answered.

🗣️ The Talking Step

Do you think there is anything God cannot forgive you for? Why?

Is there something you need to ask God to forgive you for right now?

👐 The Praying Step

Dear God, thank You for forgiving me. Thank You for loving me. Help me to obey You more.

If we tell God about our sins, he can always be trusted to forgive us and take our sins away.

—1 John 1:9

Jesus Promised to Return for the Believers

Matthew 28:16–20; Mark 16:19–20; Luke 24:50–53; Acts 1:4–12

The Thinking Step

Do you keep your promises? Do your parents always keep their promises?
   When was the last time you broke a promise?
   When was the last time you kept a promise?

The Listening Step

It was time for Jesus to leave. The disciples had spent more than three years with Him. It was time for Jesus to return to heaven. But the disciples would not be alone.

"The Holy Spirit will come upon you and give you power," Jesus told them. "I will be with you always."

As the disciples were watching, Jesus was taken up into the clouds. The disciples kept looking up into the heavens, hoping to catch one last look at Jesus.

"Why are you standing here and looking up into the sky?" voices called from behind them. The disciples turned around. Two angels were standing there.

The angels said, "Jesus has been taken to heaven. But he will come back in the same way that you have seen him go."

The disciples returned home. Jesus had promised to return someday!

The Talking Step

What are some promises God has made? Do you think God keeps His promises?
   Name some promises that God has kept.

146

🖐 The Praying Step

Dear God, thank You for all You have promised me. Thank You for keeping Your promises.

We must hold tightly to the hope that we say is ours. After all, we can trust the one who made the agreement with us.

—Hebrews 10:23

God Released Peter and the Apostles

Acts 5:12–32

The Thinking Step

Have you ever been in trouble for doing something God wanted you to do?

What happened?

The Listening Step

Peter and the other apostles told people about Jesus. Many people believed. The church was growing every day. Some people were not happy, though. They did not believe in Jesus. And they did not like Peter and the apostles talking about Jesus. They arrested the apostles and put them in jail.

When it was night, an angel opened the prison doors and let the apostles out. Then the angel said, "Go to the temple and tell the people everything about this new life."

In the morning a messenger went to those who had put the apostles in prison. He said, "Those men you put in jail are in the temple, teaching the people!"

So they arrested the apostles again. "We told you plainly not to teach in the name of Jesus," they said.

"We don't obey people. We obey God," Peter and the others answered.

God protected the apostles. They obeyed God and He took care of them.

The Talking Step

Will we still have problems if we obey God? Why? Why not?

Will God help us through our problems? How?

🖐 The Praying Step

Dear God, I know that even when I obey You, I may have problems. Help me to trust You through those times as well.

> We don't obey people. We obey God.
>
> —*Acts 5:29*

God Helped Christians Spread the Gospel Despite Enemies

Acts 7:54–8:8

The Thinking Step

Have you ever been made fun of because you believe in God?
What happened?

The Listening Step

After the Holy Spirit came to the disciples in the Upper Room, they started telling people about Jesus. They even healed the sick and performed miracles, just like Jesus had done.

But some people did not want the disciples telling people about Jesus. Those people told the disciples not to tell anyone about Jesus. Stephen, a new disciple, was arrested because he told people that Jesus was God's Son. Some people became so angry, they threw stones at Stephen and killed him. Soon some people were going into homes and dragging Christians to jail.

The Christians ran for their lives. They scattered everywhere. And everywhere they went, they told people about Jesus. The gospel message about Jesus was being spread. The persecution turned out to be good. It sent the story about Jesus around the world!

The Talking Step

Why does God allow bad things to happen?
Describe a time you saw God turn something bad into something good.

🖐 The Praying Step

Dear God, thank You for watching over me, even during the hard times. I know You are in control of all things. Thank You for making good out of bad.

> In everything we have won more than a victory because of Christ who loves us.
>
> –Romans 8:37

Jesus Converted Saul

Acts 9:1–9

 The Thinking Step

Who led you to Christ?

Could you become a Christian without someone telling you about Jesus?

The Listening Step

Saul loved God very much. But he did not understand about Jesus. He did not believe Jesus was God's Son. So Saul wanted to stop the Christians from talking about Jesus.

One day Saul decided to go to Damascus. He wanted to see if any Christians were there talking about Jesus. He was going to arrest them and put them in jail. But something happened on the way to Damascus that changed Saul's life forever.

Saul was getting near Damascus when a bright light knocked him to the ground. Then he heard a voice, "Saul, Saul! Why are you so cruel to me?" It was Jesus! But Saul did not know who He was.

"Who are you?" he asked. "I am Jesus. I am the one you are so cruel to," Jesus answered.

When Saul opened his eyes, he could not see a thing. His friends led him by the hand to Damascus. From then on, Saul knew that Jesus was God's Son.

The Talking Step

Would God allow you to keep disobeying Him? Why? Why not?

How might He show you that you are not doing the right thing?

152

✋ The Praying Step

Dear God, sometimes I get discouraged. I need You to encourage me. Help me to listen for Your encouraging words. Help me to listen to others You may send to encourage me.

> We should keep on encouraging each other to be thoughtful and to do helpful things.
>
> —*Hebrews 10:24*

God Saved Paul

Acts 27

The Thinking Step

When was the last time you had to make a hard decision? What did you do?

Who helped you make the right decision?

The Listening Step

Paul was finally on his way to Rome. He had wanted to go to Rome for a long time. But he was going as a prisoner.

The ship set sail for Rome with Paul and other prisoners on board. The weather was very rough, and the ship had a hard time on the water. The captain of the ship and his crew were worried about keeping everyone safe.

Then one night an angel appeared to Paul. "Don't be afraid, Paul!" the angel said. "God will save the lives of everyone on the ship."

So the captain decided to guide the ship to an island. As he did, the ship was broken up by the waves. Everyone grabbed a piece of the ship and floated to safety.

God told Paul what would happen so Paul could help the captain make the right decision.

The Talking Step

Name a time God helped you make the right decision. How did He help you?

Could God use others to help you make a good decision? How?

✋ The Praying Step

Dear God, I want to do what You want me to do. Please help me make the right decisions. Help me to know the right thing to do.

> You, LORD God, are my mighty rock and my fortress. Lead me and guide me, so that your name will be honored.
>
> *–Psalm 31:3*

God Helped Paul in Rome

Acts 28:11–31

The Thinking Step

When was the last time you dreaded doing something?
   Did it turn out to be as awful as you thought it would be? Or better?

The Listening Step

Paul was going to Rome. He was a prisoner for telling people about Jesus. Paul did not know what was going to happen. Many prisoners were killed in Rome. Paul knew that could happen, too. When Paul got to Rome, he wrote to his good friends, the Philippians, "If I live, it will be for Christ, and if I die, I will gain even more."

   Soon after arriving in Rome, Paul asked to meet with the religious leaders. He explained to them about Jesus and told them that Jesus was God's Son, the Messiah. Paul stayed in his own rented house and told everyone about Jesus. Many people came to see Paul in his house. He was able to talk about Jesus in Rome, just as God had promised!

The Talking Step

Is God in control of everything that happens? Can He make bad things good things?
   Name a time you expected something to be bad and God turned it into something good.
   When bad things happen, what should we do?

158

🖐 The Praying Step

Dear God, sometimes I dread doing certain things and going certain places.
Help me to trust You more. Help me not to dread doing hard things.

> With all your heart you must trust the LORD and not your
> own judgment.
>
> —*Proverbs 3:5*